THE GIANT How to Catch ACTIVITY BOOK for KIDS

BASED ON THE *NEW YORK TIMES* BESTSELLING SERIES FROM ADAM WALLACE & ANDY ELKERTON

sourcebooks wonderland

Published by Sourcebooks Wonderland, and imprint of Sourcebooks Kids.
P.O. Box 4410, Naperville, Illinois 60567–4410
(630) 961-3900
sourcebookskids.com

Source of Production: PrintPlus Limited, Shenzhen,
Guangdong Province, China
Date of Production: March 2021
Run Number: 5021015

Printed and bound in China.

PP 10 9 8 7 6 5 4 3 2 1

TABLE OF CONTENTS

COLORING — 4

HIDDEN PICTURE — 28

HOW TO DRAW — 50

TRAPS & ACTIVITIES — 70

DOT-TO-DOT — 92

SPOT THE DIFFERENCE — 106

MAZES & COMPLETE THE STORY — 118

SOLUTIONS — 141

CERTIFICATE — 159

The monster's parents are actually quite tame, can you find the baby in the picture frame?

Our favorite thing to do
at the beach is jog,
can you find our loyal dog?

COLOR THE PAGE AND READ THE RHYME FOR EXTRA FUN!

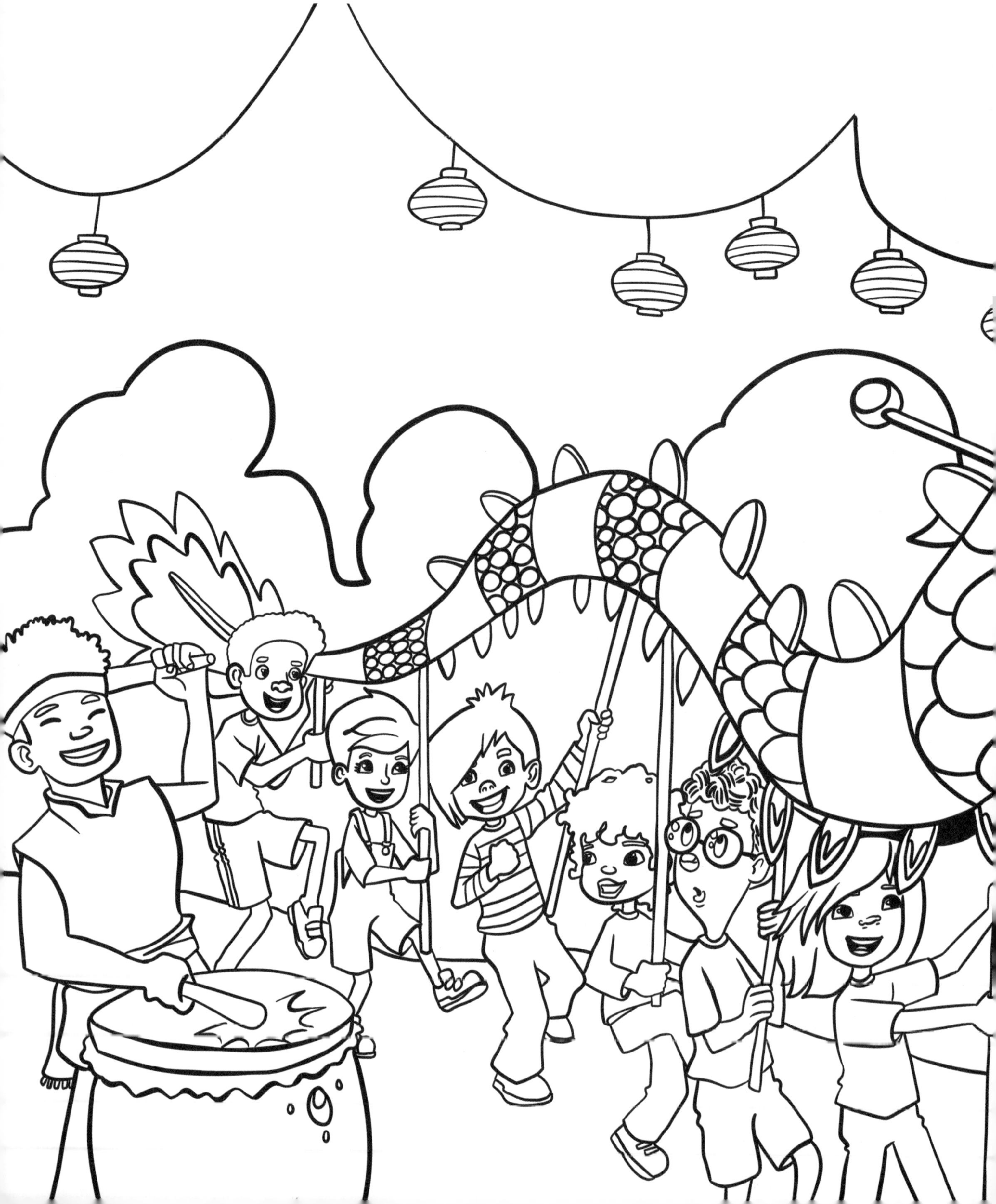

As the elf flies through the sky, can you find the pizza pie?

COLOR THE PAGE AND READ THE RHYME FOR EXTRA FUN!

While the kids are distracted and focused on their prize, can you find the dino dressed in disguise?

Wow! The yeti family has grown!
Can you find the yeti with the hair bone?

Spring always comes
with lots of rain showers,
can you spot four
blooming flowers?

CAN YOU CATCH SIGHT OF THESE HIDDEN PICTURES?

- [ ] A PAIR OF GOGGLES
- [ ] A GINGERBREAD MAN
- [ ] A RED FEATHER
- [ ] A TOOTH UNDER A PILLOW
- [ ] A PINEAPPLE
- [ ] BUBBLE GUM

CAN YOU CATCH SIGHT OF THESE HIDDEN PICTURES?

- [ ] A TAPE MEASURE
- [ ] A CANDLE HOLDER
- [ ] FOUR BLUE FEATHERS
- [ ] THREE MARKERS
- [ ] A CARROT
- [ ] A ROBOT

- [ ] TWO GOLD COINS
- [ ] A SPOOL OF THREAD
- [ ] A SMILEY FACE
- [ ] THREE MUDDY PAWPRINTS
- [ ] TWO TONGUES
- [ ] A LEMON

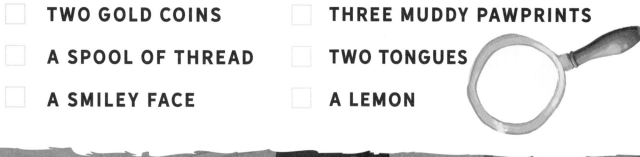

CAN YOU CATCH SIGHT OF THESE HIDDEN PICTURES?

- [ ] **THREE GOLD COINS**
- [ ] **THE LETTER** *H*
- [ ] **TEN HANDPRINTS**
- [ ] **THREE TOILET PAPER ROLLS**
- [ ] **TWO BEAKS**
- [ ] **THREE FISH**

CAN YOU CATCH SIGHT OF THESE HIDDEN PICTURES?

Snowman Accessories

- [ ] A HEART
- [ ] TWO WHITE STARS
- [ ] FOUR BANANAS
- [ ] THREE BIRDS
- [ ] A MIRROR
- [ ] A LADYBUG

CAN YOU CATCH SIGHT OF THESE HIDDEN PICTURES!?

- [ ] A BOOK
- [ ] THREE YELLOW EGGS
- [ ] A BLUE RIBBON
- [ ] A STARFISH
- [ ] A TIARA
- [ ] TWO BOOTS

- [ ] A DRAGON
- [ ] TWO BOTTLES OF GLUE
- [ ] A RED CRAYON
- [ ] A PINK MARBLE
- [ ] A PENCIL
- [ ] A NEEDLE

- [ ] A STAR
- [ ] A GOLD CROWN
- [ ] NINE TURKEYS
- [ ] NUMBERS 1–5
- [ ] A MARKER
- [ ] AN APPLE

CAN YOU CATCH SIGHT OF THESE HIDDEN PICTURES?

A WATCH

A BLUE CANDY CANE

A PAIR OF GLASSES

TWO PURPLE CRAYONS

A LOLLIPOP

A SPOON

- [ ] THE LETTER Q
- [ ] FOUR HEARTS
- [ ] A UNICORN HORN
- [ ] THREE TOOTHPASTE TUBES
- [ ] A KEY
- [ ] A CROWN

CAN YOU CATCH SIGHT OF THESE HIDDEN PICTURES?

- [ ] A PUPPY SNOUT
- [ ] A GREEN MARBLE
- [ ] A MUSHROOM
- [ ] PAINTBRUSH WITH ORANGE PAINT
- [ ] THREE FROSTED CUPCAKES
- [ ] AN ALLIGATOR

Ready for an extra challenge? Go back and look through the hidden pictures to find twenty-five green shamrocks!

Totally a UNICORN

FOLLOW THESE FUN STEPS AND LEARN HOW TO DRAW!

1
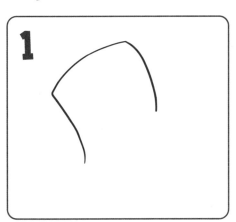

2
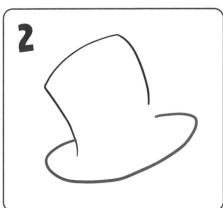

3

4
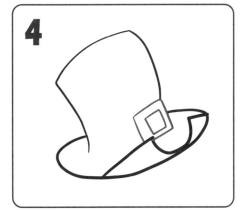

5

6

7

8

9

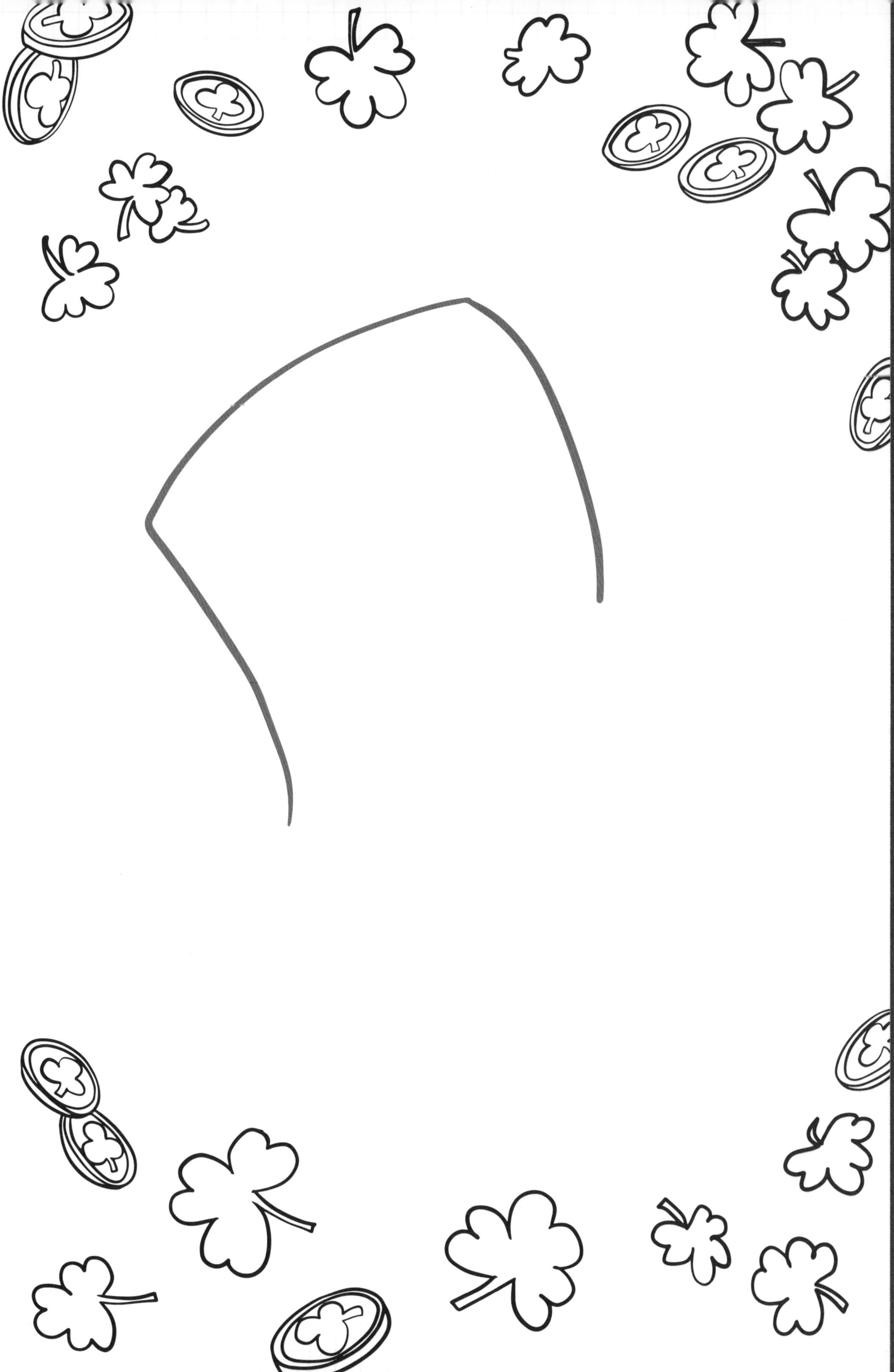

FOLLOW THESE FUN STEPS AND LEARN HOW TO DRAW!

1

2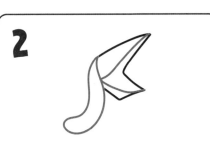

3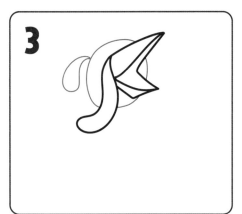

4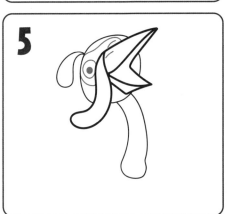

5

6

7

8

9

FOLLOW THESE FUN STEPS AND LEARN HOW TO DRAW!

1

Draw this step very lightly.

2

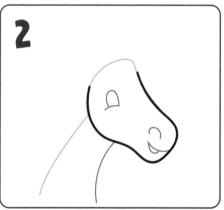

3

4

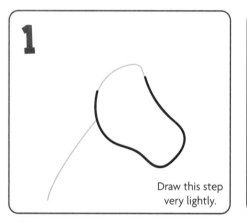

5

6

7

8

9

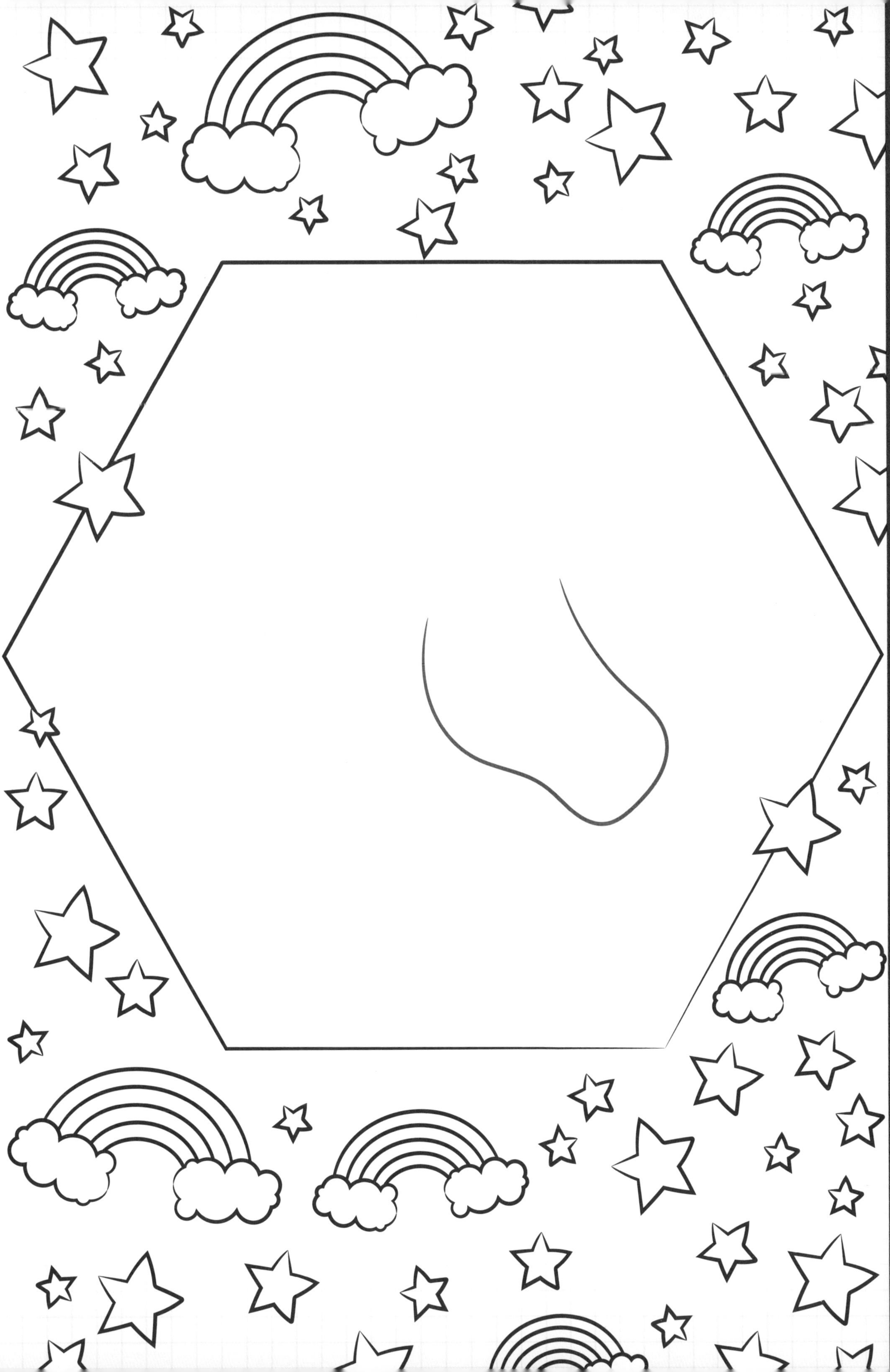

FOLLOW THESE FUN STEPS AND LEARN HOW TO DRAW!

1
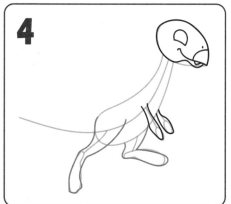
Draw this step very lightly.

2
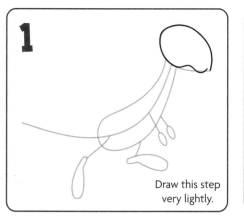

3

4

5

6

7

8

9

FOLLOW THESE FUN STEPS AND LEARN HOW TO DRAW!

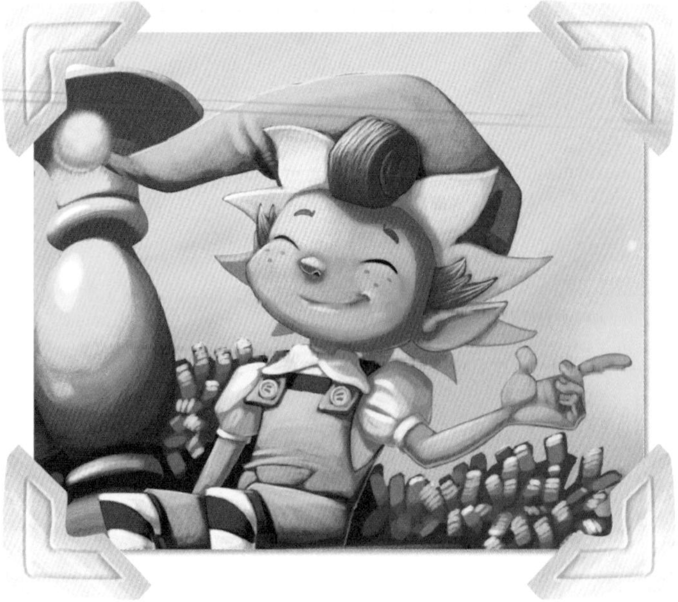

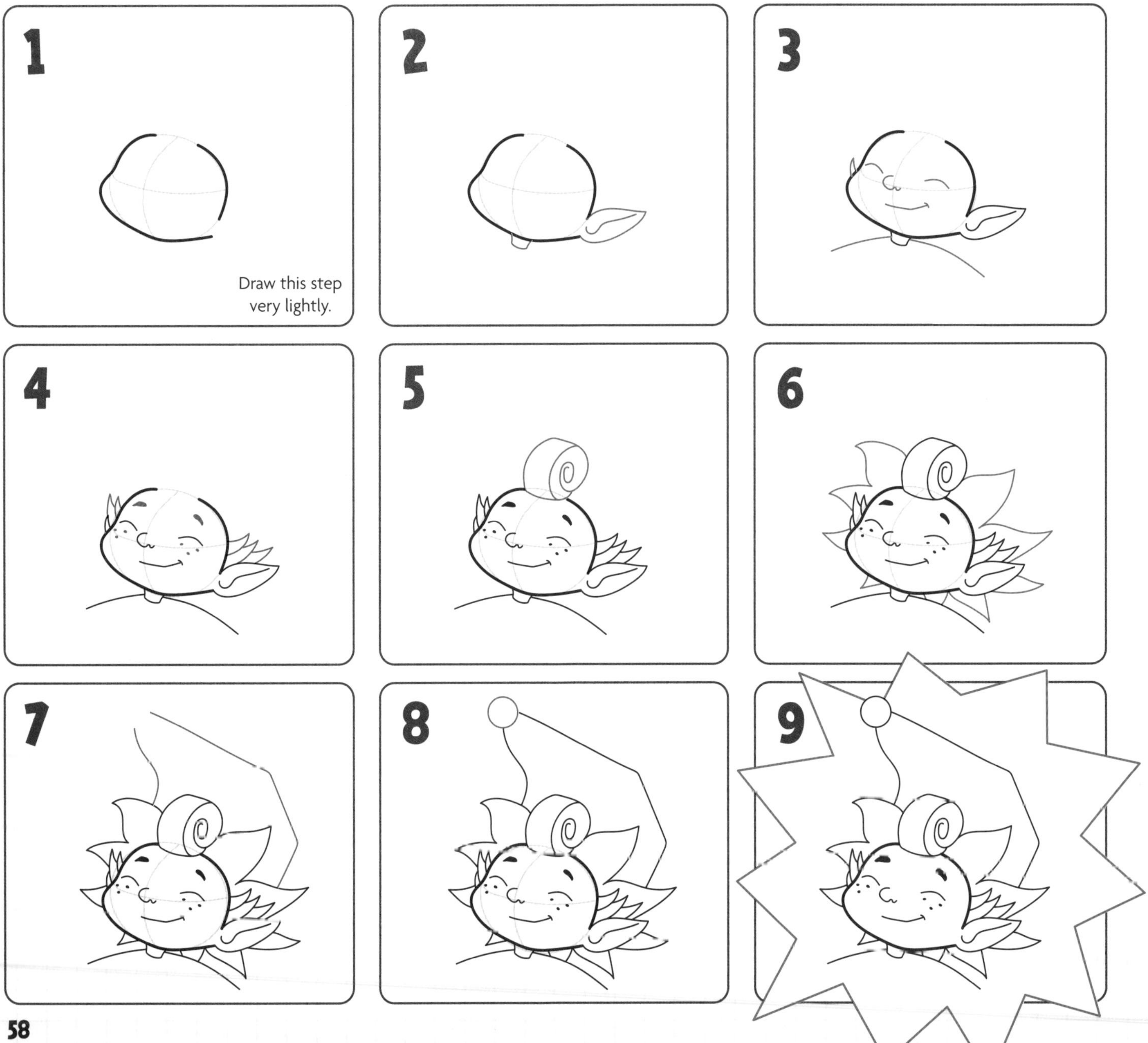
1
Draw this step very lightly.
2
3
4
5
6
7
8
9

FOLLOW THESE FUN STEPS AND LEARN HOW TO DRAW!

1

Draw this step very lightly.

2

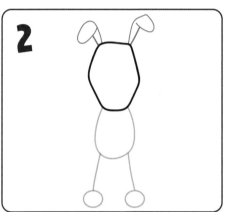

3

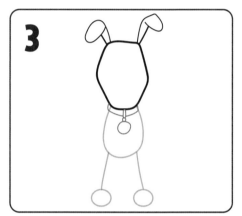

4

5

6

7

8

9

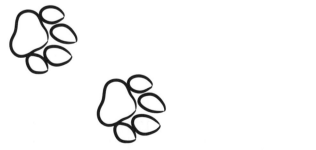

FOLLOW THESE FUN STEPS AND LEARN HOW TO DRAW!

1

Draw this step very lightly.

2

3

4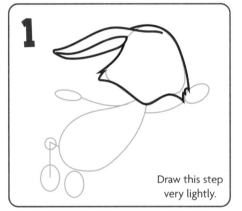

5

6

7

8

9

FOLLOW THESE FUN STEPS AND LEARN HOW TO DRAW!

1

Draw this step very lightly.

2

3

4
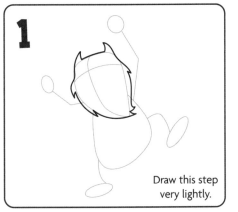

5

6

7

8

9

FOLLOW THESE FUN STEPS AND LEARN HOW TO DRAW!

1

Draw this step very lightly.

2

3

4

5

6

7

8

9

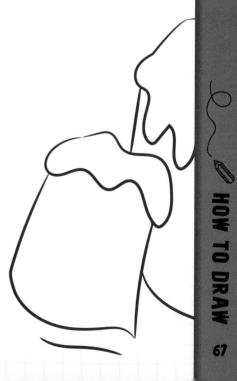

FOLLOW THESE FUN STEPS AND LEARN HOW TO DRAW!

1

Draw this step very lightly.

2

3

4

5

6

7

8

9

TURKEY SNATCHER 500

Try this fun activity to help you trap a turkey!

DIFFICULTY: ✂ ✂

MATERIALS

- Large square box—big enough to hold a basketball
- Scissors or craft knife*
- Construction paper
- Tape
- Screwdriver*
- Spool of ribbon
- Foam board
- Colored markers
- Self-adhesive magnet strip (optional)

*Requires parental supervision

STEAM CONNECTION

A drawbridge is a heavy, movable bridge that could be raised during attacks for protection. Castle defenders could lift one end of the bridge into the air by hoisting up chains or ropes and sealing the drawbridge against the side of the castle like a huge door. Drawbridges were very heavy, so there was usually a counterweight (a really heavy object) to help pull up the bridge. In this trap, the fake-food lure acts as both the counterweight and the bait for our turkey! Once it pulls on the lure, it will apply force to the drawbridge (and ribbons), which will close shut. The magnet adhesive lining the edges will apply extra pressure to the door to ensure it stays closed.

DIRECTIONS

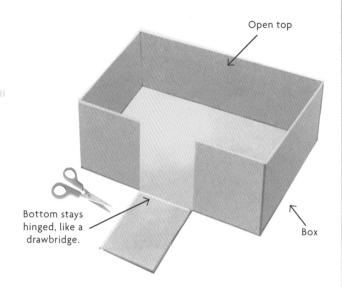

Open top

Box

Bottom stays hinged, like a drawbridge.

1 With <u>adult supervision</u>, cut out a large door on the base of your box, leaving the bottom part attached like a hinge so it opens and closes vertically—this will be your drawbridge. Turkeys can vary in size, so your door doesn't have to be exact!

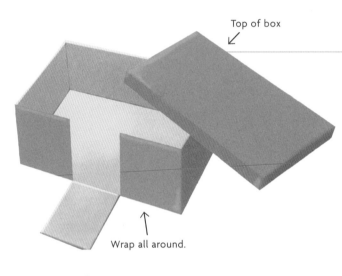

Top of box

Wrap all around.

2 Cover the top and bottom of your box with construction paper and secure with tape. Make sure to cut and fold the paper carefully around the door!

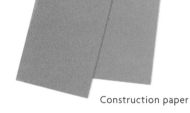

Tape

Construction paper

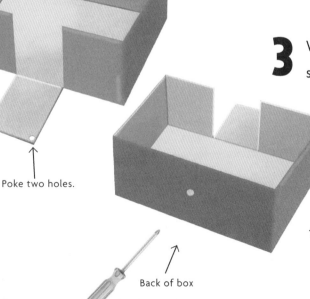

Poke two holes.

Back of box

3 With <u>adult supervision</u>, use a screwdriver to poke one hole each through the top two corners of the drawbridge. Poke another hole in the center of the back of the box—this should be the opposite side of the door.

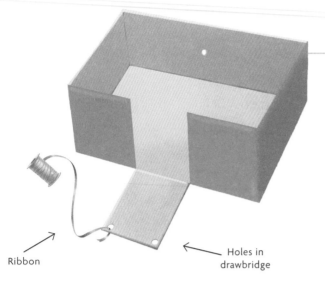

Ribbon

Holes in drawbridge

4 Cut two long strands of ribbon and thread each one through the two top holes of the drawbridge. Knot each end of each ribbon so they don't pull through the hole.

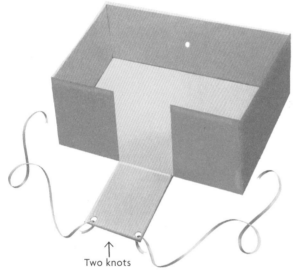

Two knots

DID YOU KNOW?

Wild turkeys are actually very fast! They can run up to 25 miles per hour and even fly as fast as 55 miles per hour! Also, turkeys love to eat nuts like acorns, as well as leaves, fruit, and seeds!

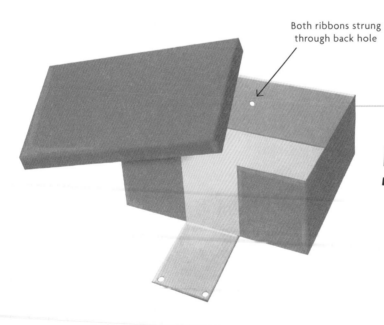

Both ribbons strung through back hole

5 Put the lid on the box. Bring the pieces of ribbon over the top of your box and push them into the back hole so they are inside your trap.

6 Create a tasty lure for the turkey by cutting a medium circle out of foam board and drawing acorns or leaves on it.

Foam board

Markers

7 With <u>adult supervision</u>, punch two holes through the foam board, side by side.

Poke two holes.

8 Take the two dangling ribbon ends from step 5. Thread and knot them through the holes in the foam board. Once your turkey pulls this down— **SNAP!** The ribbon will pull the door shut!

Optional: Take four pieces of self-adhesive magnet and line the door and entryway to ensure that it will stay closed.

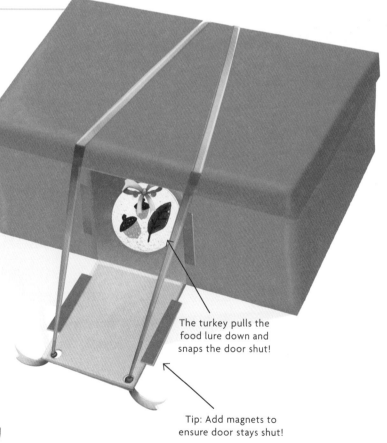

The turkey pulls the food lure down and snaps the door shut!

Tip: Add magnets to ensure door stays shut!

Self-adhesive magnet

WALKING RAINBOW

Try this fun activity to help you trap a unicorn!

DIFFICULTY:

MATERIALS

- 6 mason jars
- Red, blue, and yellow food coloring
- Paper towels
- Water

STEAM CONNECTION

Color mixing and capillary action are at the center of this activity. What is capillary action? This is a process that occurs when water flows through the surface of other materials without the aid of any tools or manipulation—and this phenomenon is precisely what goes on in this activity. Vary the amount of water in the jars, mix colors, switch out cups, and use different kinds of paper toweling (does one-ply or two-ply paper allow the colors to travel faster?). Changing up *variables* (things that change in an experiment) can affect the outcome of your experiment!

DIRECTIONS

1 Fill three jars with water and leave the other three empty.

2 For the jars with water in them, add several drops of red food coloring to one jar, blue to the second jar, and yellow food coloring to the third.

3 Form a circle with your six jars, alternating empty and colored jars.

4 Roll up paper towels into long cylinder shapes. Place one end of a cylinder into a full jar and the other end into the adjacent empty jar. *Repeat this step until each jar has two paper towel ends in it.*

5 **PATIENCE ALERT!** This process will take about two days, but keep checking on it to watch the colors appear.

PREHISTORIC SUCCULENTS

Try this fun activity to help you lure a dinosaur!

DIFFICULTY: ✂ ✂

MATERIALS

- 6 small pots/planters
- Shallow dish or paper plate
- Small bag of potting soil
- 6 tiny succulent plants
- Paintbrush
- Paint
- Paper towels

STEAM CONNECTION

Succulent plants are extra special because they have shallow roots and absorb water more quickly than other plants, which help them survive in the dry heat of the desert. Succulent plants such as cacti, aloes, and agaves survive the lack of water and intense heat by storing plenty of water in their roots, stems, or leaves, which is why they do not need to be watered often. Since succulents can be tricky, keep a log of when you water the plants. After a few months have passed, look back at your log to see if certain seasons require the plants to be watered more frequently than others.

DIRECTIONS

1 Pour paint in a shallow dish or paper plate.

2 Place your pots upside down on paper towels.

3 Gently dip the paintbrush into the paint and paint rock, lava, or dinosaur footprint patterns on your pots. Let dry.

4 Once your pots are dry, flip right side up and fill two-thirds up with potting soil.

5 Make a little hollow for the roots by scooping the potting soil to the side with your fingers.

6 Gently press your succulents' roots into the potting soil and pat down soil around them.

Depending on your succulent plant variety and size, they will need around a tablespoon of water about once a week.

DID YOU KNOW?

Herbivore dinosaurs had broad, flat teeth perfect for stripping plants! *Xiaosaurus* was an herbivorous dinosaur that lived in Asia during the Jurassic period. Its fossils have been discovered in the Chinese province of Sichuan!

CANDY CRUNCH

Try this sweet treat to help you lure the Easter Bunny!

DIFFICULTY: ✂ ✂

INGREDIENTS

- Plain popcorn, popped*
- Pretzels, chopped*
- Plain rice cereal squares
- Mini marshmallows
- White chocolate chips
- Rainbow sprinkles
- Pastel-colored milk chocolate candies

*Requires parental supervision

STEAM CONNECTION

Measuring is key in this activity. But not measuring with a ruler—we're using a measuring cup. For this recipe, it is up to you to come up with the measurements—start with half a cup of each ingredient and experiment with how different ratios of ingredients make this recipe sweeter, saltier, or crunchier. There is no wrong combination; just keep in mind that the more ingredients you add, the more Candy Crunch you'll have for the Easter Bunny, friends, and family!

DIRECTIONS

1 Spread popcorn, pretzels, rice cereal squares, and marshmallows on a parchment-lined baking sheet.

2 With adult supervision, use a microwave or double boiler to melt the white chocolate chips. Use a spoon to drizzle the melted chocolate on top of the snack mix.

3 Scatter the pastel chocolate candies and sprinkles on top of the white chocolate drizzle.

4 Refrigerate for half an hour to solidify the white chocolate drizzle.

Note: You can substitute peanuts for popcorn, or raisins for marshmallows and make it trail mix style!

MINI FAIRY TERRARIUM

Try this fun activity to help you trap the Tooth Fairy!

DIFFICULTY: ✂ ✂

MATERIALS

- Mason jar with lid (preferably with removable lid disk insert)
- 1 cup sand
- 1 cup tiny rocks or pebbles (often called pea gravel)
- 1 cup potting soil
- 1 sheet card stock
- 1 packet grass or clover seeds
- Pencil
- Tablespoon
- Decorations

Decorations add a cute touch to your terrarium, but they have to be tiny and can get wet and humid. Little ceramic bunnies, fairies, or flowers will make your garden feel like a little piece of magic in a jar. You can also form tiny creatures or fairy cottages for your terrarium using oven-bake clay.

STEAM CONNECTION

This activity will show you the water cycle in action! After you water your terrarium, the water evaporates and droplets collect at the top of your terrarium. These droplets then drip down to nourish your plants like rain. Your garden recycles the water you provide, over and over again, which is why you only need to water them every few weeks. Be sure to look up additional information on terrarium care based on the types of plants you have and the specific conditions your plants may need. Keep track of growth and watering in a science log to determine how often you need to replenish the water in your own ecosystem.

DIRECTIONS

1 **LAYER!** Start with 1 in. of pebbles on the bottom of a clean mason jar.

2 Now add 1 in. of sand.

3 Add 1 ½ in. (approximately) of potting soil on top of the sand. Carefully use the tip of your pencil eraser to poke the soil, creating tiny little holes.

4 Sprinkle your grass or clover seed over the potting soil and dust the seeds with a tablespoon of potting soil.

5 Add decorations gently on the soil layer.

6 Sprinkle a tablespoon of water onto the dirt.

7 Take your mason jar lid (round disk) and trace its shape on your card stock. Cut this circle out and secure it onto your mason jar with the band.

8 Poke a few holes into the paper so your seeds can get air!

Water your seeds every other day with a tablespoon of water. If you start to notice mold in your jar, take the top off and let it get more air for a few days.

TEA LIGHT SNOWMEN

Try this fun activity to help you lure an elf!

DIFFICULTY:

MATERIALS

- Black felt or construction paper
- Scissors*
- LED tea lights
- Hot glue gun*
- Black puffy paint
- Small, heavy-duty magnets

  *Requires parental supervision

STEAM CONNECTION

This project uses magnets to get the tea lights to stick to the refrigerator—but how *do* they stick? Magnets have a magnetic force that flows from the magnet's north and south poles, creating a magnetic field. This field causes two magnets to attract (come together) or repel (push away). Most refrigerators have steel doors with magnetic field lines that run through the metal, so when an object with a magnetic force is near, their opposite poles attract and the two objects stick together!

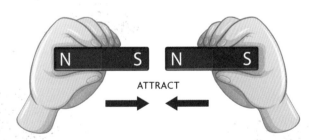

ATTRACT

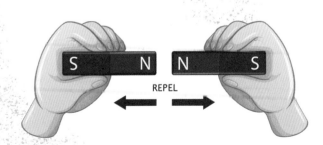

REPEL

DIRECTIONS

1 Use black felt or construction paper to cut out a top hat. With <u>adult supervision</u>, hot glue the hat to the front of the tea light.

2 Use puffy paint to make dots for the snowman's eyes and smile.

3 With <u>adult supervision</u>, hot glue the magnet to the back of the tea light.

4 Switch on your snowman's nose and display on a magnetic surface!

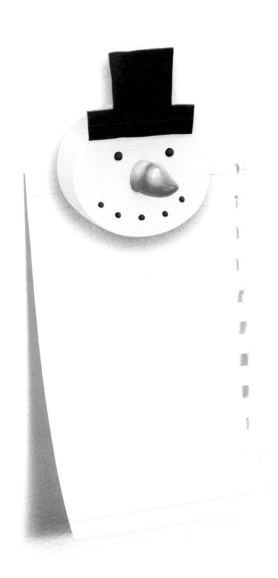

CRYSTAL SNOWFLAKE ORNAMENTS

Try this fun activity to help you catch a yeti!

DIFFICULTY: ✂ ✂

MATERIALS

- Pipe cleaners
- Scissors*
- String
- Pencil
- Jar
- 2 cups boiling water*
- 6 tablespoons Borax Laundry Booster (Caution: Do not ingest.)
- Colorful ribbon
- ***Requires parental supervision**

STEAM CONNECTION

Borax is made up of special symmetrical *molecules*, the microscopic particles that make up a substance. When Borax is added to boiling water, its molecules dissolve due to the high temperature, but as the solution cools, the Borax molecules begin to expand and attach themselves to the inserted pipe cleaner, forming crystals.

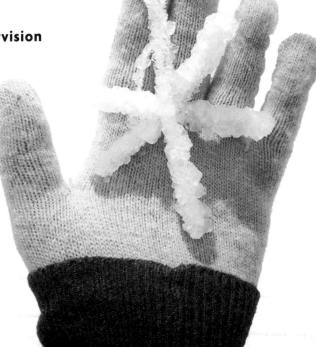

DIRECTIONS

1 With <u>adult supervision</u>, cut pipe cleaners into various sizes of strips and twist together to create a snowflake shape.

2 Tie string around the top of the snowflake tip and fasten the other end around the middle of a pencil. Place snowflake in jar with pencil resting across the top.

> *Tip: Make sure the pipe cleaners do not touch the sides of the glass!*

3 With <u>adult supervision</u>, dissolve Borax into boiling water and pour into jar.

4 Let snowflake sit in the solution for twenty-four hours. Keep checking back to watch the crystals form!

5 Once set, remove the snowflake from the jar and let dry. Then, tie a ribbon to the snowflake.

This is a sticky trap that could help you catch a yeti. When you're finished using the crystal snowflake as a trap, you can use it as an ornament!

Pipe cleaners

String

Pencil

MINI WINDMILL

Try this fun activity to help you lure a leprechaun!

DIFFICULTY: ✂ ✂

MATERIALS

- Small paper cup
- Scissors*
- Nontoxic acrylic paint

- Construction paper, variety of colors
- Craft glue
- 1 brad

*Requires parental supervision

DIRECTIONS

1 Paint small paper cup. Let dry.

Small paper cup

Paint

2 With <u>adult super-vision</u>, cut out two fan blades from construction paper, about 1/2 x 2 in. Glue into a criss-cross, one on top of the other.

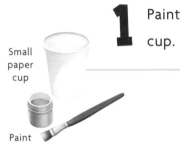

8½ x 11 in. construction paper

½ in.

2 in.

3 Turn your cup upside down. Carefully poke a brad through the center of your crisscrossed fan blades and the cup, toward the top of the windmill.

Inside of cup

Sides of brad pushed down

Paper cup (upside down)

½ x 2 in. strips of construction paper

Brad

4 Push down sides of the brad inside the cup. Spin your fan blades around!

SOMEWHERE OVER THE MAGIC RAINBOW

Try this fun activity to help you catch a unicorn!

DIFFICULTY:

MATERIALS

- Hot glue gun*
- Glue stick
- Scissors*
- Box lid
- Glittery construction paper in rainbow colors (or make your own in Step 1)
- Cotton balls
- Marshmallow cereal (or other rainbow cereal)
- Craft stick (or other device to prop up box lid)

   *Requires parental supervision

STEAM CONNECTION

Time to put your engineering caps on! This trap uses a craft stick to prop up the lid that will catch our unicorn when it shrinks in size, and it's up to you to figure out which angle works best for the stick and lid. Experiment with the angle of the stick and where you position it against the lid to see which option will hold up the longest and snatch the unicorn the quickest!

DIRECTIONS

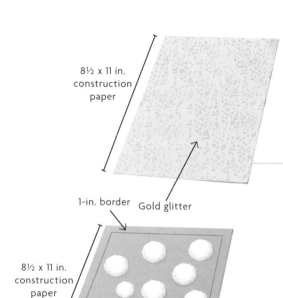

8½ x 11 in. construction paper

1-in. border   Gold glitter

8½ x 11 in. construction paper

Cotton balls

1 **GLITTER ALERT!** If you already have glitter construction paper, this will be used for your cut-out gold coins later on. If you don't have glitter paper already, spread glue all over construction paper and sprinkle with gold glitter. Shake off excess and let dry.

2 Grab your glue stick again! This time, spread glue on another piece of paper and stick cotton balls all over it, leaving a 1-inch border.

3 Cut 5 x 1 in. strips of construction paper to create a rainbow path. Glue each colored strip to the top border of the cotton-ball paper.

5 x 1 in. strips of construction paper

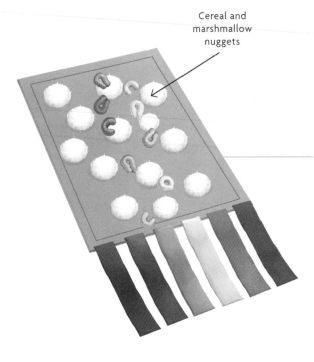

Cereal and marshmallow nuggets

4 Sprinkle marshmallow cereal nuggets on top of the cotton balls. (Your unicorn won't be able to resist this rainbow-cloud path to sugary goodness!)

8½ x 11 in. glitter paper from step 1

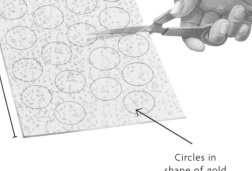

5 With adult supervision, cut out coins from your glitter paper to add to your cloud in the next step.

Circles in shape of gold coins

DID YOU KNOW?

A rainbow is formed by light reflecting off raindrops! Raindrops act like a prism when they are in the air. When light enters a water droplet, it bounces off the back of the water droplet and reflects at angles, causing the light to bend. This process allows you to see different colors!

6 Wrap the box lid in colored construction paper. Prop up the lid with a craft stick (with its other end on the cotton-ball cloud) to create a **SNAPPITY SNAP TRAP** when your devious little unicorn tries to eat its marshmallows!

Shoebox lid

Craft stick

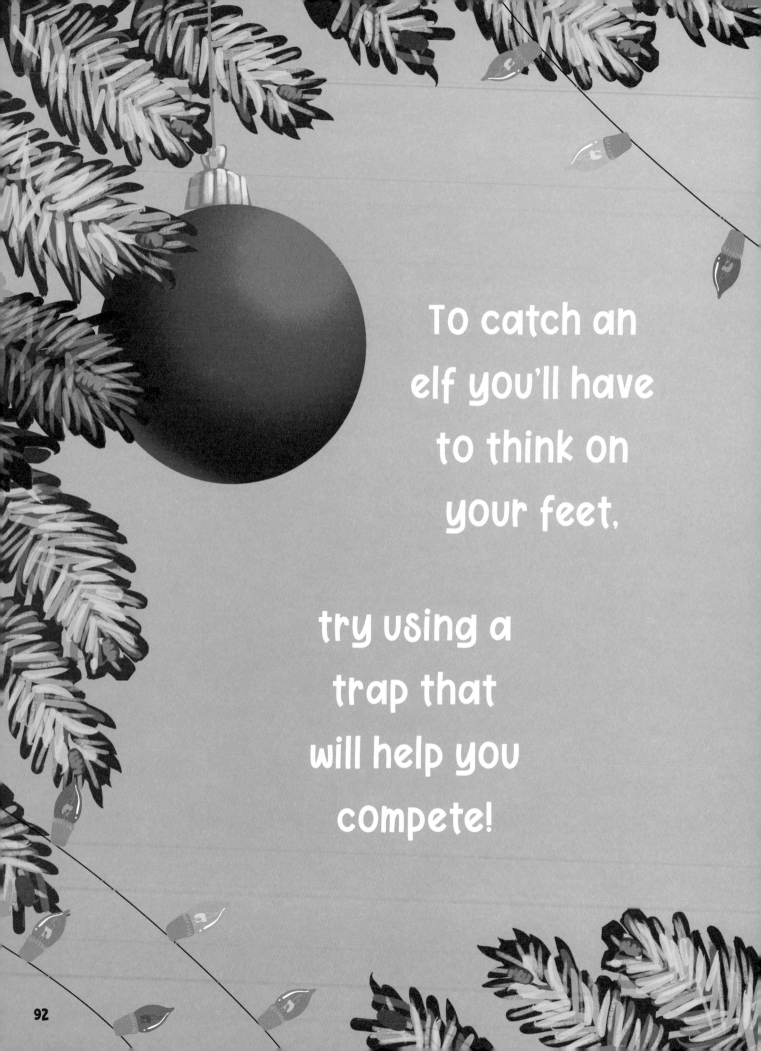

To catch an
elf you'll have
to think on
your feet,

try using a
trap that
will help you
compete!

CONNECT THE DOTS TO REVEAL A TRAP!

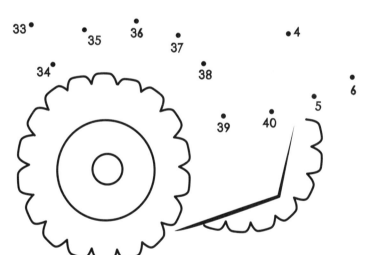

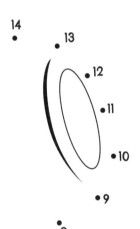
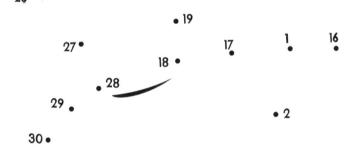
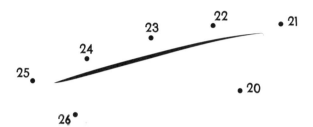

To catch a mermaid
in your trap,
use something
that can snap!

CONNECT THE DOTS TO REVEAL A TRAP!

To catch a leprechaun
you'll need to be quick,

try using a trap that
snaps with a click!

CONNECT THE DOTS TO REVEAL A TRAP!

To trap a monster you've got to put up a fight,

try something with teeth that is blue and white!

CONNECT THE DOTS TO REVEAL A TRAP!

1 2 3 6 7 8 9 10 11 12 13
4 5
60
14
58 59
15
57
21 20 19 18 16
22 17
56
23
55
54 24
41 30
42 35 25
40 36 34 26
53 43 37 27
38 33 29 28
52 39 31
51 44 32
50 45
48
49 47 46

To trap a Yeti you can't go wrong,
use a machine that is
smart and strong!

CONNECT THE DOTS TO REVEAL A TRAP!

1 2 3 4
15 14
16 13
17 12 5
11 80 79 78 77 76
18 75
19 6 74
7 73
10 9 8
32 60 72
20
33 59 61 71
21 31 62 70
22 30 58 63 69
23 34 57 64 68
24 29 35 56 65 66 67
28 55
25 27 36
26 37 38 54
39 46 53
40 52
41 45 47 51
42 44 48 50
43 49

Catching a dinosaur is hard to do right,

try using a plant that's got a sharp bite!

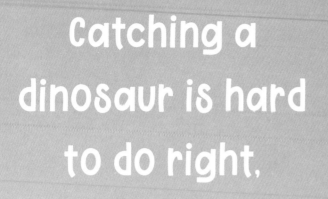

CONNECT THE DOTS TO REVEAL A TRAP!

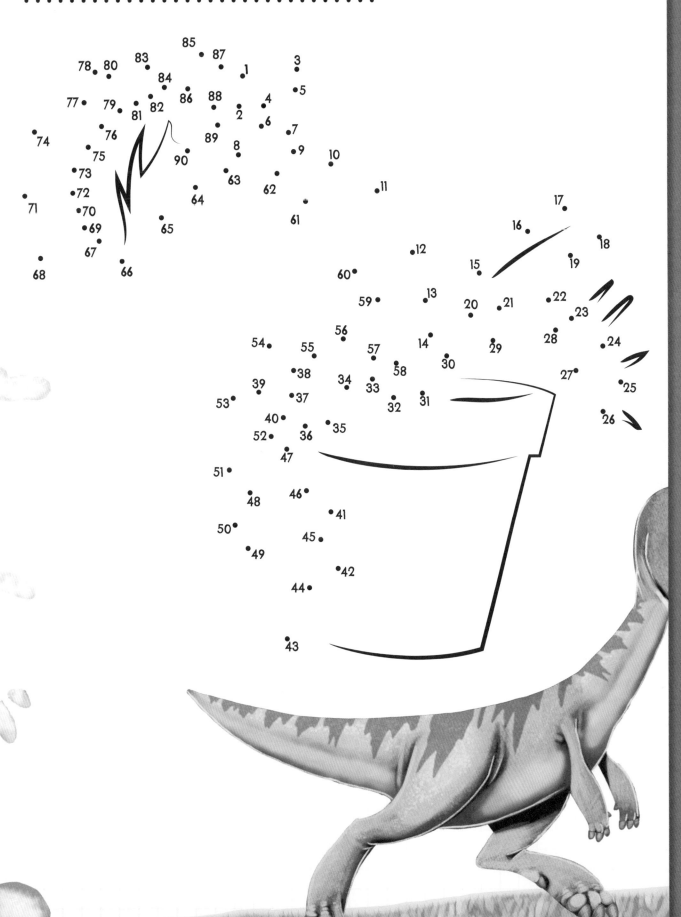

To trap a unicorn you'll have to be smart to win,

try using a beautiful home for it to live in!

CONNECT THE DOTS TO REVEAL A TRAP!

SEE CUTEST UNICORN HERE!

SEE CUTEST UNICORN HERE!

CAN YOU CATCH THE **5** DIFFERENCES BETWEEN THESE PICTURES? TURN THE BOOK TO START SEARCHING!

CAN YOU AVOID THE BOOKCASES AND FURNITURE TO HELP THE CATCH CLUB KIDS CATCH THE TURKEY?

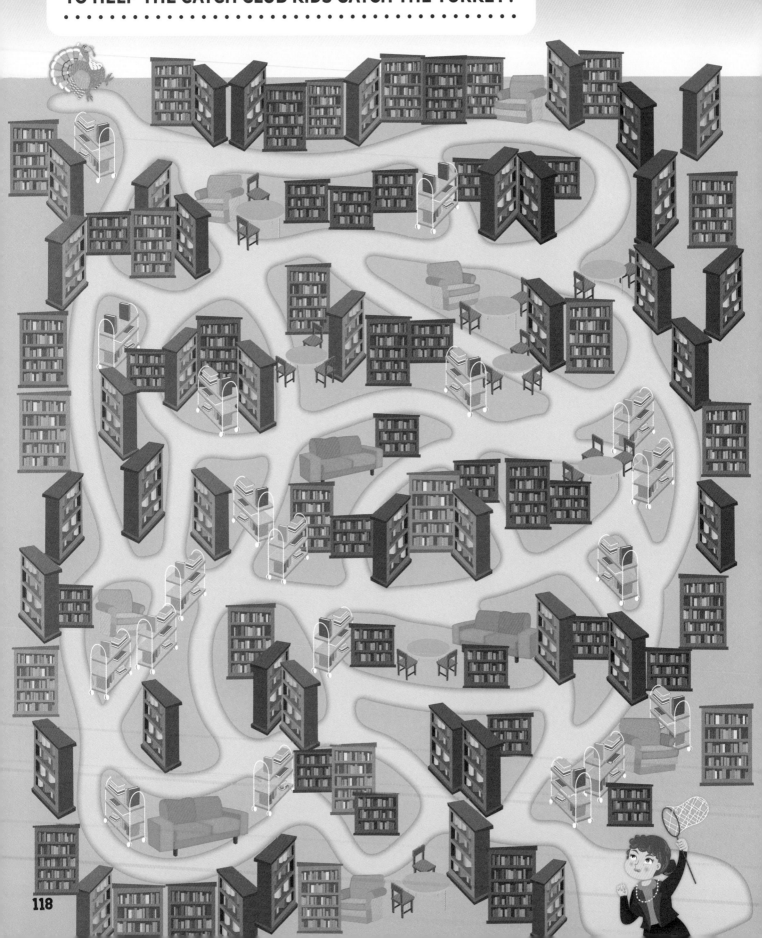

COMPLETE THE STORY WITH A FRIEND OR MAKE THE SILLIEST STORY EVER AND SHARE WITH A FRIEND LATER!

Finally the kids gave up, but the principal gave chase. My only hope of escaping her was _____ _____ _____ _____ !

(complete the story)

I burst into the _____

(describing word) room,

knocked over _____ and _____ ,

(object) (object)

and the cry of, "Catch that turkey!"

boomed over the loudspeakers.

CAN YOU AVOID THE SEA CREATURES AND CORAL TO HELP THE CATCH CLUB KIDS CATCH THE MERMAID?

COMPLETE THE STORY WITH A FRIEND OR MAKE THE SILLIEST STORY EVER AND SHARE WITH A FRIEND LATER!

Our mermaid comes to save the day!

She made a trap to save us.

She scares the sharks by _____

_____

_____

_____!

(complete the story)

But *how* to catch a mermaid?

You don't learn this in school.

We'll need to build a _____ trap
(describing word)

and start near the _____.
(place)

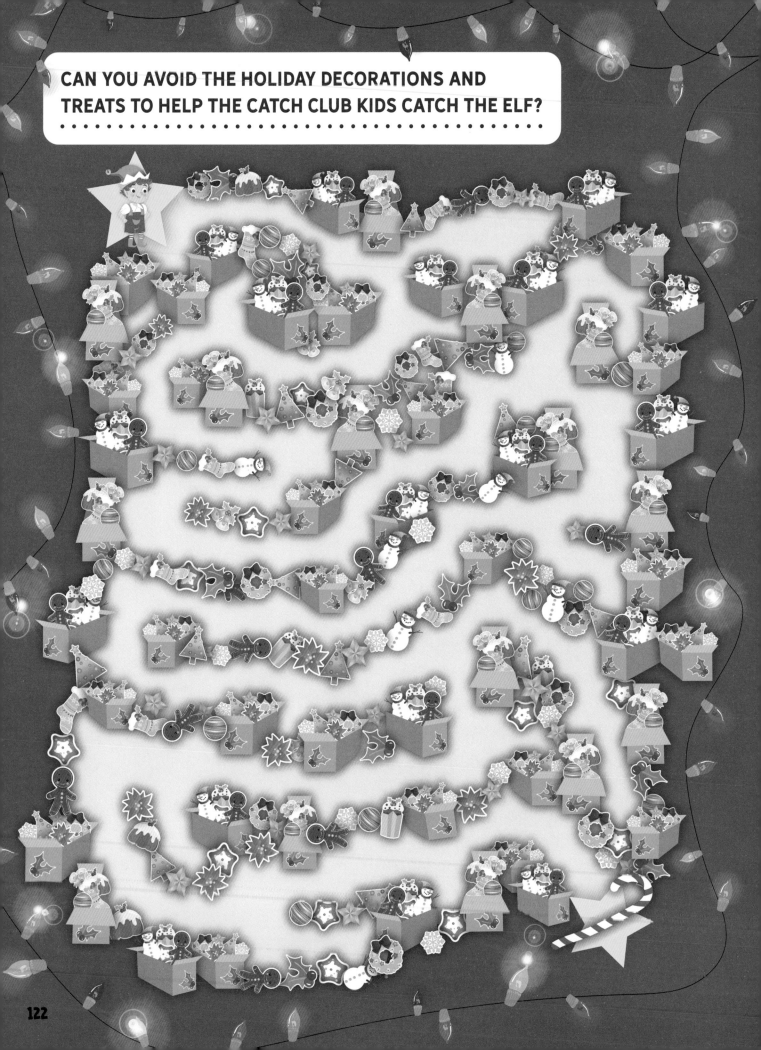

COMPLETE THE STORY WITH A FRIEND OR MAKE THE SILLIEST STORY EVER AND SHARE WITH A FRIEND LATER!

Another house is filled with _____.
(object)

These kids are getting _____!
(describing word)

I can't resist the _____.
(object)

My job is getting harder!

We run inside and get caught up in an avalanche of food!

We've seen all kinds of traps before, but not _____

_____

_____!
(complete the story)

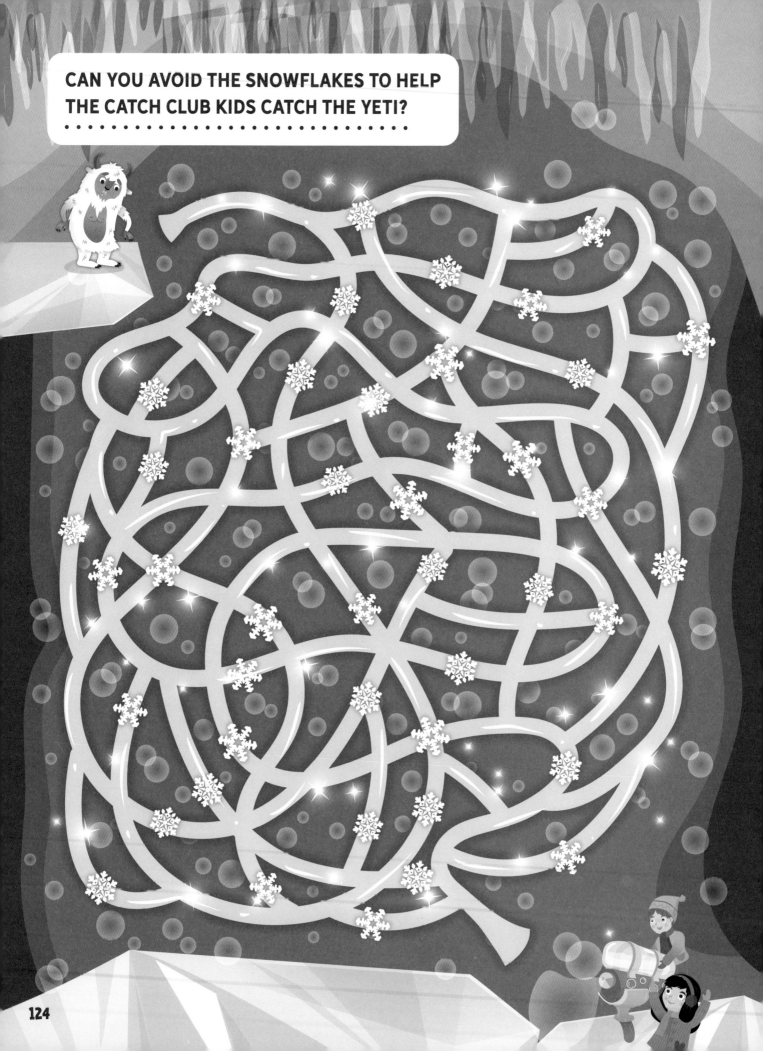

CAN YOU AVOID THE SNOWFLAKES TO HELP THE CATCH CLUB KIDS CATCH THE YETI?

COMPLETE THE STORY WITH A FRIEND OR MAKE THE SILLIEST STORY EVER AND SHARE WITH A FRIEND LATER!

We thought that marbles, sleds, and _____
(object)
would finally do the trick.

But Yeti's moves are off the charts!

That dude is really _____!
(describing word)

I thought for sure that this would work,

But the yeti got away.

I've got an idea that just can't lose.

It's _____

_____

_____!
(complete the story)

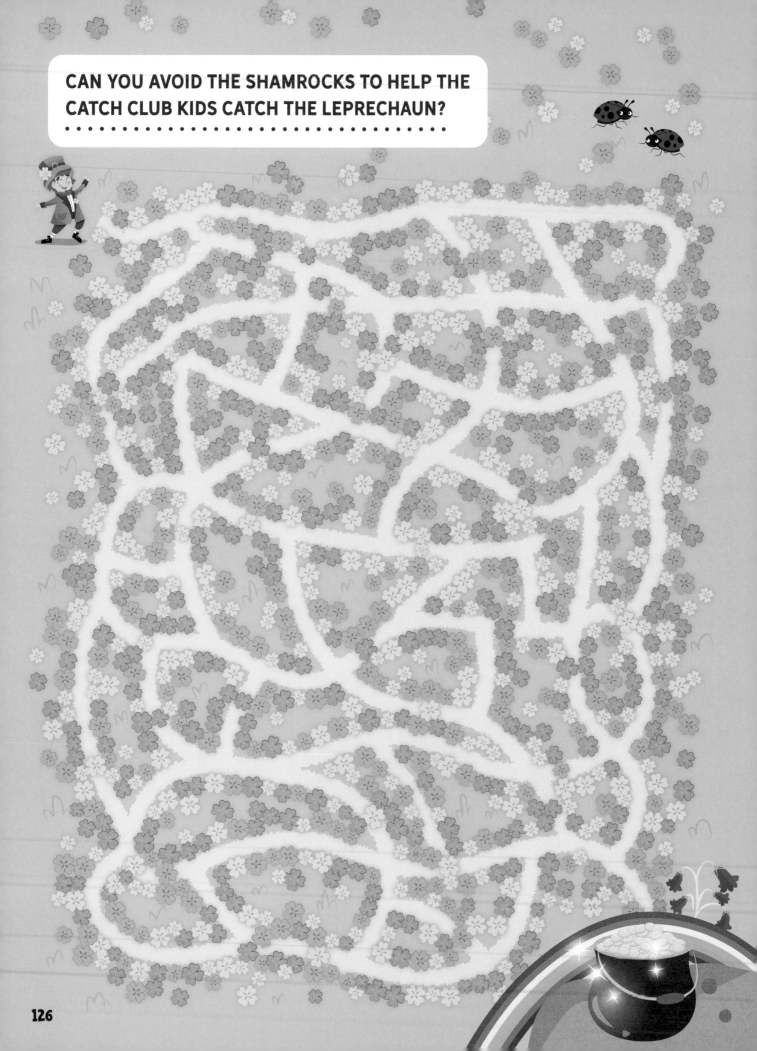

CAN YOU AVOID THE SHAMROCKS TO HELP THE CATCH CLUB KIDS CATCH THE LEPRECHAUN?

COMPLETE THE STORY WITH A FRIEND OR MAKE THE SILLIEST STORY EVER AND SHARE WITH A FRIEND LATER!

Another house. I fixed your shoes!

They really were quite _____!
(describing word)

I'll eat the _____ you left as bait
(object)

and leave with a full belly.

The Leprechaun Be Gone 3000

gave me quite a scare.

But without a four-leaf clover,

_____

_____

_____

_____!
(complete the story)

COMPLETE THE STORY WITH A FRIEND OR MAKE THE SILLIEST STORY EVER AND SHARE WITH A FRIEND LATER!

The kids think they have spotted me—

I thought I'd blend in here!

I cannot let them catch me

or my magic will _____

_____

_____!

(complete the story)

I dodge the _____ parachute
(describing word)

being launched from down below.

I do a spin and leave a trail

of _____ as I go.
(describing word)

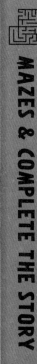

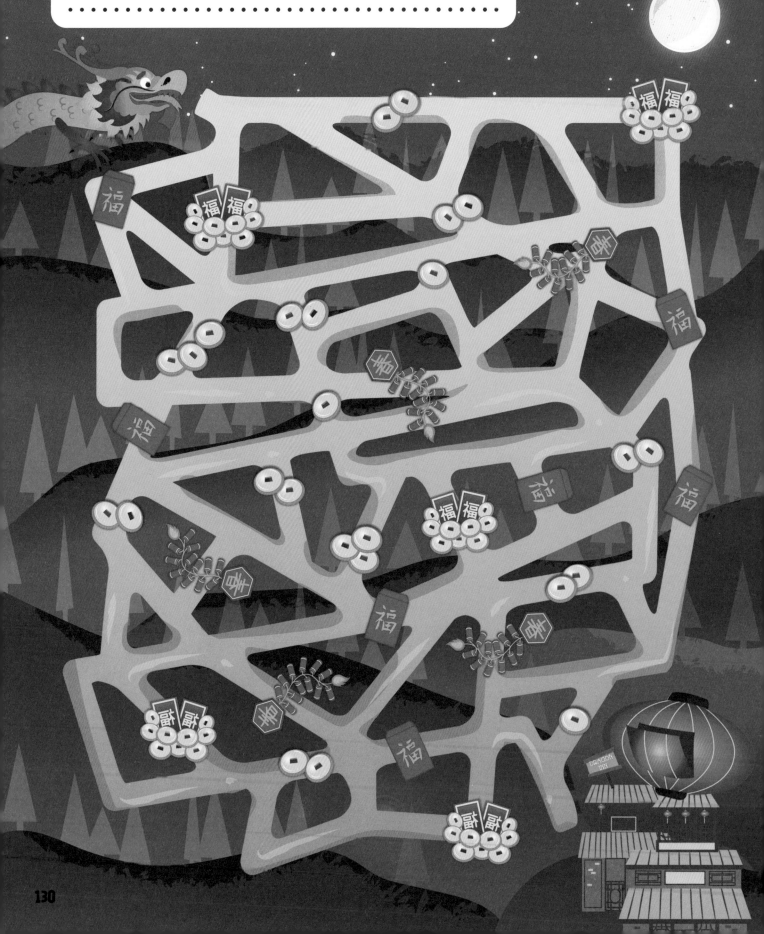

CAN YOU AVOID THE GOLD AND FIREWORKS TO HELP THE CATCH CLUB KIDS CATCH THE DRAGON?

COMPLETE THE STORY WITH A FRIEND OR MAKE THE SILLIEST STORY EVER AND SHARE WITH A FRIEND LATER!

This dragon can control

_____?
(object)

He's _____ than we thought!
(describing word)

We'll have to be much smarter

to get this dragon caught!

We cannot lose this dragon now,

not with this massive bait!

A dragon can't resist some gold.

We'll catch him _____

_____

_____!
(complete the story)

CAN YOU AVOID THE CARROTS AND SCARVES TO
HELP THE CATCH CLUB KIDS CATCH THE SNOWMAN?

FREE
SNOWMAN
SNACKS

COMPLETE THE STORY WITH A FRIEND OR MAKE THE SILLIEST STORY EVER AND SHARE WITH A FRIEND LATER!

You built me with a carrot nose—

I think that's kind of cute.

But cuter still is trying to catch me with

_____

_____

_____ !

(complete the story)

That first trap was a good attempt,

your running made me _____.

(describing word or action word)

Your net of _____

(object)

might've done the trick,

but it's left you all in a pile!

CAN YOU AVOID THE BUILDINGS AND STREETLIGHTS TO HELP THE CATCH CLUB KIDS CATCH THE TOOTH FAIRY?

COMPLETE THE STORY WITH A FRIEND OR MAKE THE SILLIEST STORY EVER AND SHARE WITH A FRIEND LATER!

_____ has a good idea:
(name)

a trap made out of _____

_____

_____ !
(complete the story)

_____ sets a trap.
(name)

They want me in a _____.
(object)

I'll take their tooth, and then for fun,

I'll hide all of their _____!
(object)

CAN YOU AVOID THE ROCKS, PLANTS, AND WATER TO HELP THE CATCH CLUB KIDS CATCH THE DINOSAUR?

COMPLETE THE STORY WITH A FRIEND OR MAKE THE SILLIEST STORY EVER AND SHARE WITH A FRIEND LATER!

Tall enough to stop a giant,

our trap had _____, _____,
(object) (object)

and _____.
(object)

But this dino smashed it all to pieces.

She should be called T. wrecks!

This clever girl runs fast as the wind

and dodged our trap in a hurry.

But we've got more in store for her,

_____

_____

_____

_____!

(complete the story)

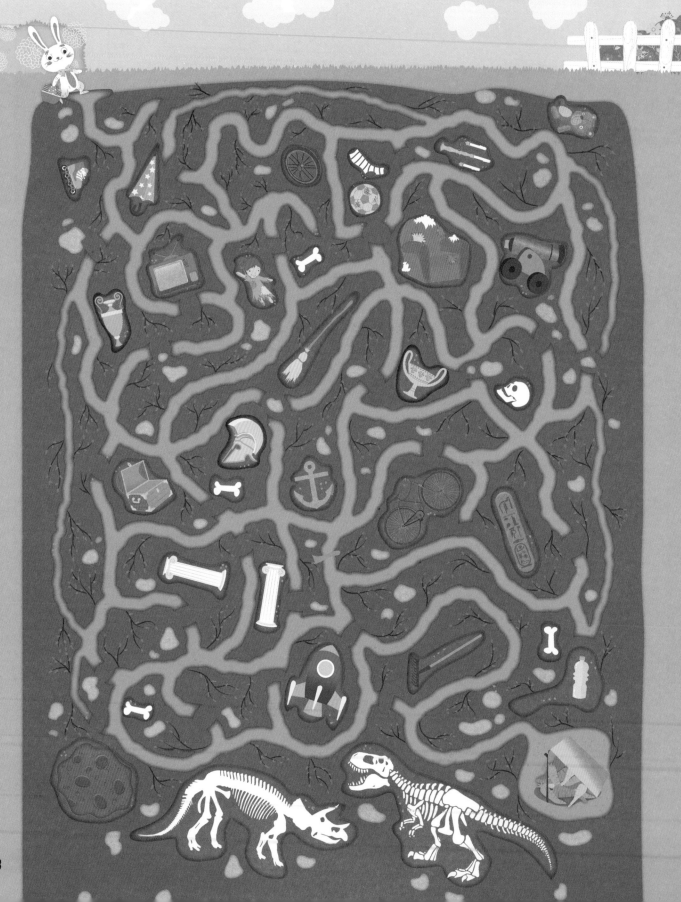

138

COMPLETE THE STORY WITH A FRIEND OR MAKE THE SILLIEST STORY EVER AND SHARE WITH A FRIEND LATER!

This first trap is quite simple,

Just _____ on a
                    (object)

_____.
                    (object)

I'm _____!
                    (describing word)

To catch me, you'll need some better bait!

This next trap is quite clever,

made by brilliant _____.
                                        (name)

But it's hard to catch a bunny who has

_____

_____

_____!
              (complete the story)

COMPLETE THE STORY WITH A FRIEND OR MAKE THE SILLIEST STORY EVER AND SHARE WITH A FRIEND LATER!

Okay, he's stronger than I thought.

But I'm not finished yet.

I'll catch him in my _____

_____

_____

_____!

(complete the story)

See, there's a monster in my closet,

with _____ and
        (object)

_____ and _____.
   (object)   (object)

And tonight, I'm going to scare him!

140

WALL OF FAME

You're almost finished! It's time
to check your answers...

HIDDEN PICTURE SOLUTIONS

From left to right: a gingerbread man, a pair of goggles, a tooth under a pillow, a pineapple, a red feather, bubble gum, shamrocks 1 and 2

From left to right: feather 1, feather 2, marker 1, a candle holder, marker 2, shamrocks 3 and 4, a tape measure, feather 3, feather 4, marker 3, a robot, a carrot

HIDDEN PICTURE SOLUTIONS

From left to right: muddy pawprint 1, a smiley face, gold coin 1, a lemon, muddy pawprint 2, gold coin 2, tongue 1, shamrock 5, muddy pawprint 3, tongue 2, a spool of thread

From left to right: handprint 1, fish 1, the letter *H*, beak 1, toilet paper roll 1, gold coin 1, handprint 2, shamrock 6, fish 2, beak 2, handprint 3, handprint 4, shamrocks 7 and 8, gold coin 2, toilet paper roll 2, shamrock 9, gold coin 3, fish 3, handprint 5, handprint 6, handprint 7, handprint 8, shamrocks 10 and 11, handprint 9, handprint 10, toilet paper roll 3

HIDDEN PICTURE SOLUTIONS

From left to right: banana 1, bird 1, bird 2, white star 1, banana 2, a ladybug, a mirror, bird 3, banana 3, a heart, white star 2, shamrock 12, banana 4

From left to right: boot 1, a tiara, yellow egg 1, a book, shamrock 13, a blue ribbon, yellow egg 2, boot 2, shamrocks 14 and 15, yellow egg 3, a starfish

HIDDEN PICTURE SOLUTIONS

From left to right: shamrocks 16 and 17, bottle of glue 1, a pink marble, a red crayon, a dragon, a needle, a pencil, bottle of glue 2

From left to right: an apple, turkey 1, a marker, turkey 2, turkey 3, a gold crown, turkey 4, turkey 5, the number two, turkey 6, the number four, turkey 7, shamrock 18, the number one, a star, turkey 8, the number five, the number three, turkey 9

From left to right: a lollipop, purple crayon 1, a spoon, shamrock 19, shamrock 20, a pair of glasses, a watch, shamrocks 21 and 22, a blue candy cane, purple crayon 2

From left to right: a unicorn horn, shamrock 23, toothpaste tube 1, heart 1, a crown, a key, toothpaste tube 2, heart 2, heart 3, the letter Q, toothpaste tube 3, heart 4

HIDDEN PICTURE SOLUTIONS

From left to right: an alligator, a mushroom, shamrocks 24 and 25, frosted cupcake 1, a green marble, frosted cupcake 2, paintbrush with orange paint, frosted cupcake 3, a puppy snout

DOT-TO-DOT SOLUTIONS

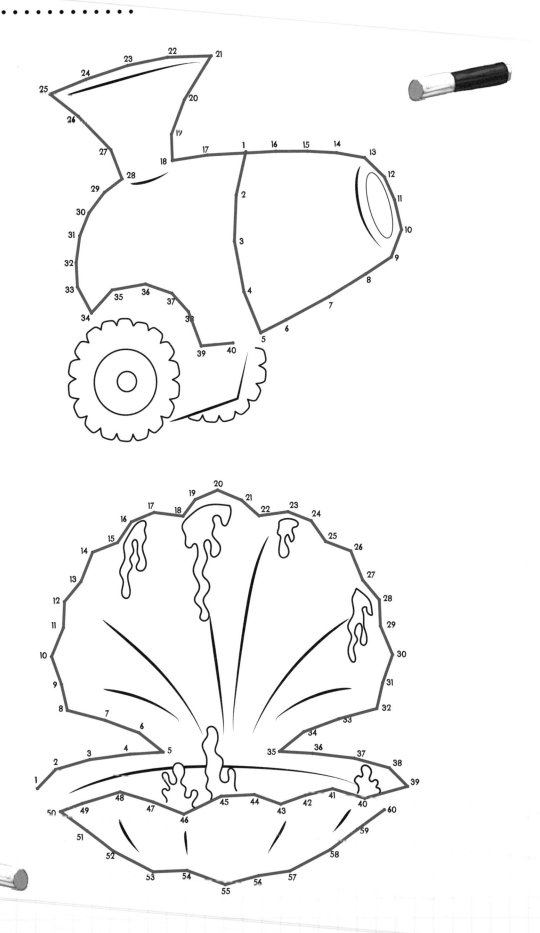

DOT-TO-DOT SOLUTIONS

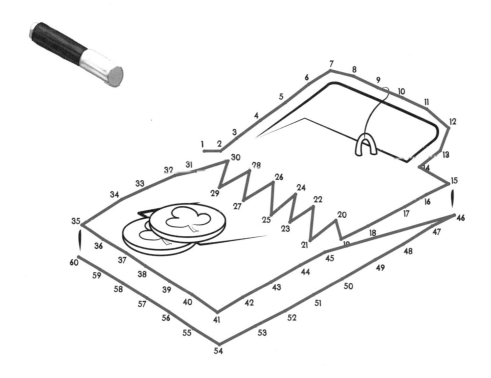

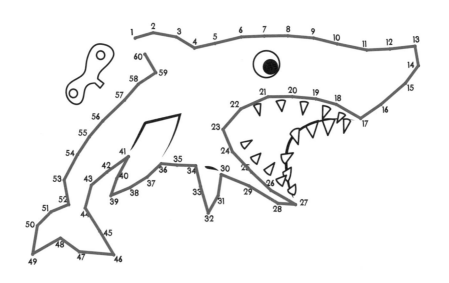

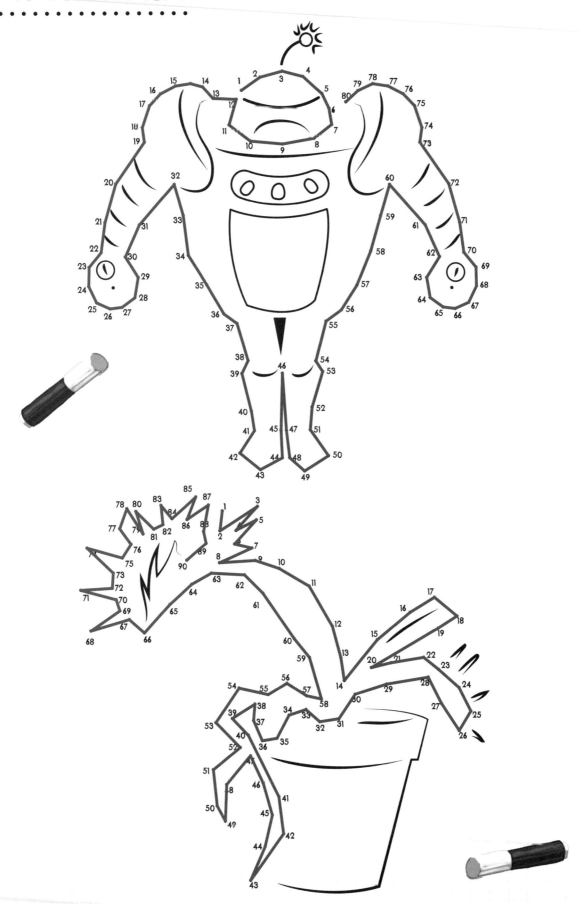

DOT-TO-DOT SOLUTIONS

SPOT THE DIFFERENCE SOLUTIONS

From left to right: book has turned green, missing clock, missing snowshoe, additional mitten, yeti face has turned purple

From left to right: toothbrush handle has turned blue, missing window, additional slipper, missing clock hand, t-shirt has turned purple

SPOT THE DIFFERENCE SOLUTIONS

From left to right: missing scroll, shirt has turned red, additional pencil, missing cat drawing, hair clip has turned pink

From left to right: missing plunger, goggles and apron have turned green, potion has turned blue, missing stripe on shirt, additional feather

SPOT THE DIFFERENCE SOLUTIONS

From left to right: sock has turned yellow, missing unicorn on shirt, missing net, additional penguin, missing flower on Unicorn

From left to right: additional flower, ribbon has turned red, missing ribbon on trunk, missing finger, missing Easter Bunny

MAZE SOLUTIONS

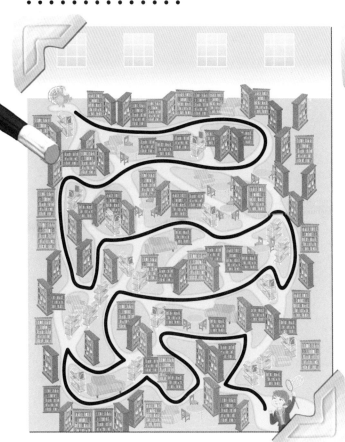

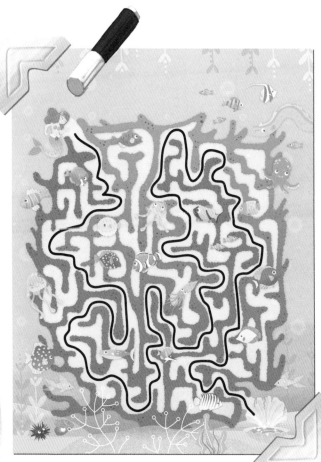

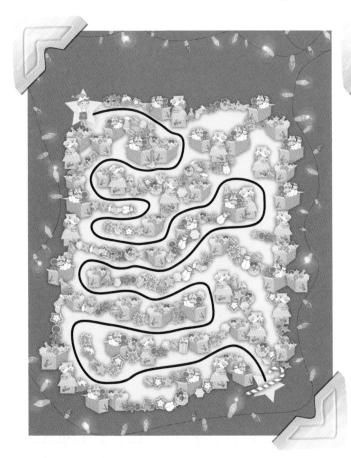

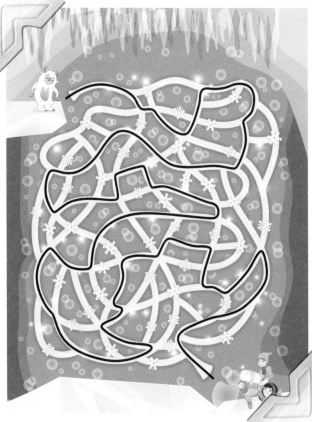

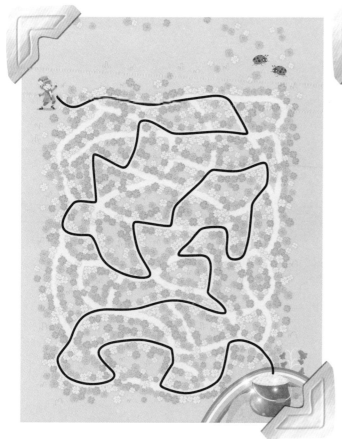

MAZE SOLUTIONS

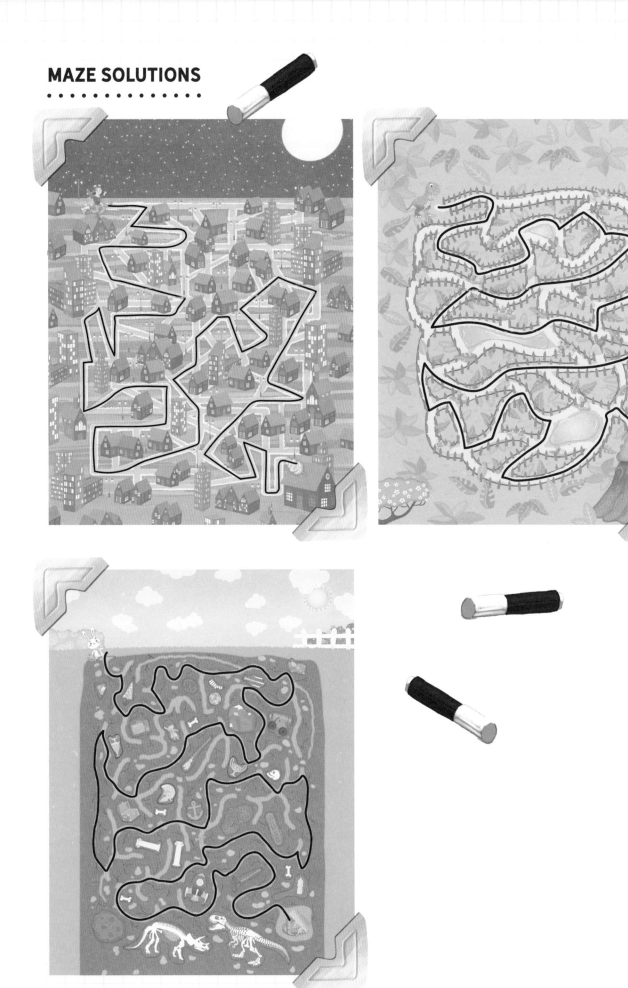

TRAP ALL THE BOOKS IN THE HOW TO CATCH SERIES!

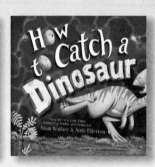

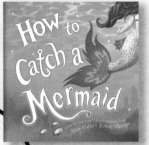
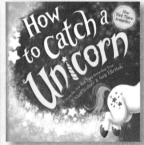

COMING SOON!

Catch more fun at
HowtoCatchClub.com!

FROM THE OFFICE OF THE

How to Catch Club

APPROVED

This prestigious certificate serves as undeniable proof of your lifetime acceptance into the How to Catch Club as a certified Creature Conservation Specialist. As a certified Creature Conservation Specialist, you are hereby granted the authority to conduct research into the whereabouts of magical creatures worldwide. Your research will be instrumental in helping the Catch Club Kids understand the magical properties of unicorns, the travel patterns of dinosaurs, the characteristics of monsters, and more, as you discover new information from your expeditions.

Set your traps, esteemed Creature Conservation Specialist, and help the Catch Club Kids catch magical creatures!

_____
Your Name

_____
Date

How to Catch Club